SEVEN, THE COMPLETION

"AND ON THE SEVENTH DAY GOD ENDED HIS WORK WHICH

HE HAD MADE; AND HE RESTED ON THE SEVENTH DAY FROM

ALL HIS WORK WHICH HE HAD MADE." GENESIS 2:2

ABOUT THE AUTHOR:

I'M A RESIDENT OF ST. LOUIS, MO. I'M A CONSULTANT AND MENTOR WITH THE FATHER FIGURES FOUNDATION. I ATTEND BELIEVERS TEMPLE WORD FELLOWSHIP UNDER THE LEADERSHIP OF BISHOP CALVIN AND PROPHETESS DEBORAH SCOTT; I'M A FORMER USHER AND FAITHFUL MEMBER. I'M ALSO CONNECTED TO THE TRUTH FORUM MINISTRY UNDER MINISTER AVA BETHEL, AS WELL AS LOVE IN THE WORLD OF CHRISTIANITY WITH OVERSEER GARRETT AND PSALMIST GINA LLOYD. I'M A STUDENT OF GRACE SCHOOL OF MINISTRY WHERE THE HONORABLE PASTOR JAMES JEFFERSON SR. IS MY INSTRUCTOR.

BOOKING INFORMATION

PHONE: 314 635 7195

FACEBOOK.COM/ 7 THE COMPLETION

EMAIL: michaelathornton7@gmail.com

TO ORDER ADDITIONAL BOOKS GO TO www.createspace.com/4357879

TABLE OF CONTENTS

CHAPTER 1: INSPIRATION

BE YOURSELF

WALK IN PURPOSE

SEVEN PRINCIPLES

CHANGE

SIMPLE

SOME PEOPLE

HUMILITY

BE YOURSELF

YOU ARE UNIQUE, SO DISTINCT THAT NO ONE COULD EVER BE LIKE YOU. REALIZE YOU ARE FEARFULLY AND WONDERFULLY MADE. CREATED WITH A PURPOSE ONLY YOU CAN FULFIL. YOU HAVE YOUR OWN THOUGHTS, LOOK, FINGERPRINTS AND DNA. BE COMFORTABLE KNOWING THAT ONLY YOU CAN BE YOU. THAT'S SO POWERFUL AND PLEASING TO KNOW. WHEN YOU LOOK IN THE MIRROR, REMIND YOURSELF OF HOW SPECIAL YOU ARE. BE CONTENT ON BEING YOU, BE WHAT GOD INTENDED FOR YOU TO BE, YOURSELF. LOVE ON YOU, LOVE YOURSELF, BE YOURSELF.

WALK IN PURPOSE

THERE IS A [PURPOSE] IN YOUR PAIN AND A [PURPOSE] TO GAIN

A [PURPOSE] IN THE PROCESS IN ALL YOU OBTAIN

THE [PURPOSE] IS TAUGHT, THROUGH THE [PURPOSE] OF LIVING

THE [PURPOSE] IS REVEALED, THROUGH THE [PURPOSE] OF GIVING

THE [PURPOSE] OF LEARNING THROUGH THE [PURPOSE] OF A LESSON

KNOWING THE [PURPOSE] OF APPLICATION IS TRULY THE BLESSING

THE [PURPOSE] THAT INSPIRES IS THE [PURPOSE] YOU SHOULD SEEK

YOUR DESTINY IS DEFINED, WHEN [PURPOSE] IS COMPLETE.

SEVEN PRINCIPLES

1. BE A PERSON OF YOUR WORD, HONOR WHAT YOU SAY.

2. TREAT OTHERS THE WAY YOU WANT TO BE TREATED, IT'S ONLY FAIR.

3. ALWAYS HAVE GOOD INTENTIONS.

4. BE MATURE ENOUGH TO ADMIT YOUR MISTAKES, WE ALL MAKE THEM.

5. BE FOCUSED AND STEADFAST.

6. PRACTICE WHAT YOU PREACH, DON'T BE A HYPOCRITE.

7. COMPLETE THE THINGS YOU START.

CHANGE

IF IT IS SOMETHING YOU CAN DO TO CHANGE OR CAUSE CHANGE DO IT.

YOU DO NOT WANT TO GO THROUGH LIFE SAYING I WISH, ONLY TO REGRET NOT DOING YOUR PART TO BRING CHANGE.

I BELIEVE WE ALL HAVE THE ABILITY TO PROMOTE CHANGE. WE HAVE TO IDENTIFY WHAT NEEDS TO BE CHANGED AND HOW TO GO ABOUT IT. TO SEE THE MANIFESTATION OF CHANGE. EVERY GREAT CHANGE- AGENT, HAD A THOUGHT BEFORE THE ACTION. THINK ABOUT THE THINGS YOU WANT CHANGED, PUT YOUR THOUGHTS INTO ACTION AND BRING FORTH THE CHANGE, WE'LL BE WAITING, LOOKING FORWARD TO SEEING YOUR IMPACT OF CHANGE.

SIMPLE

SIMPLE DOES NOT MEAN EASY. SIMPLE CAN BE DIFFICULT, BUT ATTAINABLE. SIMPLE CAN BE A VAST MAJORITY OF THINGS. THE SIMPLEST THINGS AT TIMES, WE COMPLICATE. SOME OF US HAVE SIMPLE ROLES TO FILL. HOWEVER, BECAUSE ANOTHER PERSON'S ROLE SEEMS MORE OR BETTER, WE TEND TO WANT THEIRS. DON'T BE TRAPPED BY THE COMPLEXED OR DIFFICULT. SOMETIMES DIFFICULT CAUSES DISTRACTIONS FROM THE SIMPLE. BE SIMPLE, DO SIMPLE, LIVE SIMPLE.

SOME PEOPLE

SOME PEOPLE ARE SO HAPPY AND SOME ARE SAD

SOME PEOPLE CAME TO USE YOU AND TAKE ALL THAT YOU HAVE

SOME PEOPLE LAST FOR A MOMENT, A SEASON IN YOUR LIFE

SOME PEOPLE LAST LONGER TO REMIND YOU OF WHAT IS RIGHT

SOME PEOPLE BRING ABOUT A PRESENCE THAT IS SO IRRESISTIBLE

SOME PEOPLE CAN MAKE YOU FEEL NON-EXISTENT AND INVISIBLE

SOME PEOPLE ARE UNSTABLE, BRINGING MUCH CONFUSION

SOME PEOPLE ARE LIKE A MIRAGE, FAKE LIKE AN ILLUSION

SOME PEOPLE BRING COMFORT, WITH A SIMPLE HOW ARE YOU

SOME PEOPLE REALLY DISCERN THE TRUE STAR IN YOU

SOME PEOPLE CAN TOUCH WITHIN WITH A CERTAIN APPEAL

SOME PEOPLE CAN SEE THE INNER GIFT AND HELP IT BE REVEALED

SOME PEOPLE ARE PEOPLE YOU WANT AROUND ALWAYS

AND THOSE ARE THE PEOPLE YOU KEEP ALL OF YOUR DAYS

HUMILITY

BE A PERSON WITH QUIET CONFIDENCE, NOT PUFFED UP. BE THE PERSON OTHERS RESPECT AND SPEAK VERY HIGHLY OF.

LET YOUR HUMBLENESS GO BEFORE YOU. ARROGANCE AND CONCEIT ARE BIRTHED FROM SELFISHNESS.

HUMILITY IS BEST DISPLAYED BY GIVING HONOR TO OTHERS AND NOT SEEEKING YOUR OWN. IN NO WAY WILL BEING HUMBLE AFFECTS YOUR OUTCOME AS YOU STRIVE TO ACHIEVE FOR MORE.

IT ONLY AFFECTS HOW YOU VIEW THEM, SO BE HUMBLE, AND HAVE HUMILITY.

CHAPTER 2: HEART TO HEART

ELECT LADY

LOVE LETTER

I WISH

I-LOVE-YOU

SHADOW

WOULD YOU FORGIVE ME

LET ME HEAR YOU BREATHE

MY ELECT LADY

GRACE AND ELEGANT, BEAUTIFUL AND INTELLIGENT,

DESCRIBES WHAT EVIDENT, THAT YOUR LOVE HAS NO MEASUREMENT.

MY ELECT LADY

TO THE ONE SO ENDEARING, SHOWING LOVE NEVER FEARING,

WITH EXPRESSIONS OF SINCERITY, SO BLESSED TO RECEIVE THIS CHARITY.

MY ELECT LADY

VIRTUE, HONOR, AND FAITH, HUMILITY, HUMBLE, AND GREAT,

RIGHTEOUS, SWEET, AND LOYAL, A JEWEL PRECIOUS AND ROYAL.

MY ELECT LADY

BONE OF MY BONES, FLESH OF MY FLESH,

WHEN I LOOK INTO YOUR EYES I KNOW THAT I'M BLESSED

MY ELECT LADY

GOD GAVE ME FAVOR, GOD GAVE ME YOU

[ELECT LADY] I LOVE YOU.   TO ALL WOMEN

WISHING (I WISH)

(I WISH) YOU WERE HERE TO WALK, TALK, AND HOLD YOUR HAND

(I WISH)YOU WERE HERE TO SUPPORT ME AND BE MY # 1 FAN

(I WISH) YOU WERE HERE TO SHARE A LAUGH, SMILE, AND CHUCKLE

(I WISH) YOU WERE HERE TO WATCH A MOVIE, RELAX, AND CUDDLE

(I WISH) YOU HERE WERE SO THAT WE COULD PRAY AND READ THE WORD

(I WISH) YOU WERE HERE TO GIVE YOU THE LOVE YOU SO DESERVE

(I WISH) YOU WERE HERE TO BE YOUR COMFORT, SHOULDER, AND EAR

 (I WISH) ONE DAY SOON THAT REALITY BRINGS YOU HERE

I- LOVE- YOU

(I), BEING FREE TO EXPRESS THE WAY I FEEL ABOUT YOU. I LOVE TO GIVE

OF MYSELF; TO BRING A SMILE SO BRIGHT TO YOUR FACE THAT IT OUT SHINES

THE SUN. NOT A PERSON I KNOW WILL NOT EVER BE CONFUSED ABOUT HOW

FEEL. IT IS NOT A SECRET AND I WILL TELL THE WORLD AND SHOW THAT I LOVE

YOU. (LOVE) IS AN ACTION WORD THAT SHOULD SHOW ITSELF JUST BECAUSE.

LOVE IS THE STRONGEST FORCE IN THE WORLD. IT WILL BE SHOWN IN THE

SMALLEST OF DETAILS. WITH SIMPLE THINGS LIKE SACRIFICE, BEING

UNSELFISH IN FULFILLING THE NEEDS OF OTHERS BEFORE SELF. (YOU) BEING

THE PERSON YOU ARE, BRINGS SOMETHING UNEXPLAINABLE. PURE AND

INTENTIONAL, WITH YOU, BEING THE ONLY ONE THAT CAN BRING OUT THESE

FEELINGS. YOU ARE SPECIAL IN EVERY WAY. YOU ARE A GIFT FROM HEAVEN,

YOU BEING (YOU) IS THE BEST WAY TO PUT IT. SIMPLY STATED (I- LOVE- YOU)

SHADOW

UNDER HIS SHADOW IS WHERE HE HIDES THE RIGHTEOUS

A PERFECT PLACE FOR SOULMATES, TO RUN TO LIKE US

AS PURE AS A CRYSTAL CLEAR LAKE, WITH A CONSTANT FLOW

THE PURITY OF YOUR HEART, IS HIDDEN UNDER THE SHADOW

SHADOWS ARE TRUE REFLECTIONS OF THE PEOPLE THEY REFLECT

SHADOWS ARE UNIQUE WITH AN ILLUMINATING EFFECT

SO WHAT DOES YOUR SHADOW SAY ABOUT YOUR INDENTITY

DOES IT DRAW OTHERS TO AFFIMRM THE AFFINITY

IF   MY SHADOW EVER FADES AND SLOWLY DISAPPEARS

I KNOW AL L IS WELL, WHEN YOUR SHADOW IS CLOSELY NEAR

SO I 'LL BE IN HIS PRESENCE AND UNDER HIS SHADOW

IF I FIND YOU THERE, THEN I'LL KNOW

. . . . .THAT YOU'RE MY SHADOW.

WOULD YOU FORGIVE ME

THOUGHTS OF THE PAST AS I REFLECT BACK,
HAS ME THINKING HOW I COULD HAVE DONE THAT.
REMEMBERING THE DAYS YOU WANTED TO TALK,
HOW I ACTED SO SELFISH AND WOULD GO AND WALK

AWAY LEAVING YOU TO JUST SIT AND WAIT.
TO WONDER WHAT I'M DOING, LIKE I'M SO GREAT.
WOW, YOU REAP WHAT YOU SOW IN THIS LIFE YOU LIVE,
ASKING YOU THIS DAY, WOULD YOU PLEASE FORGIVE

I PRAY TODAY STARTS YOUR HEALING PROCESS
HOW COULD I CURSE THE VERY ONE I SHOULD' VE BLESSED
USING LOVE AGAINST YOU, TO LIFT MYSELF IN PRIDE
TO DROP MY SEED IN YOU THEN RUN AWAY AND HIDE

IMMATURE AND ARROGANT, WITH FALSE INTELLIGENCE,
HAS ME IN A PLACE OF FEELING THIS EMBARRASSMENT.
I HURT AND WOUNDED THE HEART I WAS SUPPOSED TO PROTECT,
INSTEAD, I CHOSE TO HARM, ABUSE, AND NEGLECT.

I KNEW THAT IT HURT AND THOUGHT SO WHAT,
FINALLY CAME TO ME, WHEN YOU LEFT ME STUCK.
LONELY, NOW I SIT AND WAIT BY THE PHONE
HOPING BUT KNOWING YOU WON'T CALL, BECAUSE YOU'VE MOVED ON.

WOKE UP AND REALIZED, I'M THE WRONG GUY
HOPE YOU MET ANOTHER, MUCH BETTER THAN I
COULD EVER BE TO YOU, THAN ME IN LIFE,
WISHING HIM WELL, HAVING A FAITHFUL DEVOTED WIFE

TO SUM IT ALL UP, I HOPE YOU UNDERSTAND
THESE DAYS I'M SAVED NOW AND A CHRISTIAN MAN.
IF I COULD I WOULD TAKE ALL OF THE PAIN AWAY
 SO BECAUSE I CAN'T, I' LL JUST SIMPLY SAY_____ [WOULD YOU FORGIVE ME]

LET ME HEAR YOU BREATHE

I'M REALLY A SIMPLE A MAN, THERE IS JUST A FEW THINGS I NEED

WAITING ON MARRIAGE TO TOUCH YOU, BUT I NEED TO HEAR YOU BREATHE

SEE, A BREATH REPRESENTS LIFE AND WITHOUT IT LIFE DOES NOT EXIST

TO REALLY FEEL ALIVE THAT SIMPLE SOUND I CANNOT MISS

AS I LAY DOWN TO REST, AND BEFORE I FALL ASLEEP

THE THOUGHT OF HEARING YOU BREATHE, MAKES MY REST SO SWEET

IT GIVES ME STRENGTH TO PUSH, WHEN OTHERWISE I CANNOT GIVE

WITHOUT HEARING A SIMPLE BREATH, MY EMOTIONS CANNOT LIVE

PLEASE   (LET ME HEAR YOU BREATHE)

LOVE LETTER

AM I DREAMING YET AGAIN, THAT THE SEASON WILL FINALLY MANIFEST

MY HEART YEARNING TO FIND MY SPECIAL ONE AND GIVE HER ALL MY BEST

I HAVE WAITED AND SEARCHED FOR YOU, SINCE I WAS VERY YOUNG

PLEASE HEAR ME WHEN I CALL, SAYING MICHAEL I'M THAT ONE

I'M EMPTY, I'M NOT WHOLE BECAUSE YOU'VE YET TO APPEAR

THERE'S A HOLE IN MY SIDE, WHERE YOU'LL RESIDE AND END ALL MY FEAR

THIS IS PURELY FROM MY HEART, TRANSPARENT ABOUT BEING ALONE

IT'S YOU THAT'S MISSING, YOU I NEED THAT WILL MAKE MY HOUSE A HOME

WHERE ARE YOU? WHERE ARE YOU? PLEASE SHOW ME THE LOCATION

I CAN'T WAIT ON THE DAY WE CELEBRATE, THIS JOYFUL OCCASION

SEE I HAVE CRIED MANY A NIGHTS, SILENT TEARS ALL BY MYSELF

THOUGHTS OF FEELING THE PAIN, SUFFERING FROM LONLINESS

SO THIS IS MY HONEST PLEA, FOR YOU TO MAKE MY LIFE BETTER

WHOLEHEARTEDLY ANTICIPATING, YOUR ANSWER FROM MY LOVE LETTER

CHAPTER 3: MOTIVATION

BECAUSE YOU'RE MY BROTHER

I WILL NOT QUIT

WE CAN DO IT

SOUND THE ALARM

MOTIVATION

MOTIVATED

WHO ARE YOU? WHAT ARE YOU?

BECAUSE YOU'RE MY BROTHER

I   WILL NOT BE FOOLISH,   NOR CONTROLLED BY ANGER OR RAGE

NEITHER WILL I BE ENVIOUS AND COVET THE SUCCESS YOU HAVE MADE

I WILL NOT ALLOW MYSELF TO BE SELFISH AND BE AS OTHERS

INSTEAD I CHOOSE TO CELEBRATE, BECAUSE YOU'RE MY BROTHER

SEE, THE MOST IMPORTANT RACE IS THE ENTIRE HUMAN RACE

SO LETS BAND OURSELVES IN LOVE, TO OVERCOME THE HATE

WILLING TO HELP WHEN WE CAN, ONE MAN TO ANOTHER

BEING ACCOUNTABLE TO EACH OTHER, BECAUSE YOU'RE MY BROTHER.

I WILL NOT QUIT

IN A PLACE WITH MOUNTAINS AND HILLS ARE ALL AROUND, WHEN LIFE BATTLES YOU WITH UPS AND DOWNS, WHERE LACK AND FAILURES SEEM TO ABOUND, YES IS NOT THERE, AND THE NO IS PROFOUND .

I WILL NOT QUIT

WHEN I'M THE ONLY ONE THAT STILL BELIEVES, THE ONLY ONE THAT CHOOSES TO SEE, A CHANGE COMING THROUGH ALL THE MISERY, WHILE BEING EXPOSED TO A HARSH REALITY.

I WILL NOT QUIT

WHEN THE TASK IS TALL AND THE MISSION IS LONG, TAKING ALL THAT I HAVE AND I CAN'T GO WRONG, REACHING TO THE DEPTH OF MY WILL WHEN IT'S ALMOST GONE , TO ENCOURAGE MYSELF THAT I MUST GO ON.

I WILL NOT QUIT

TO ACCEPT DEFEAT AS MY PORTION AND SHARE, IN TIMES WHERE I'M DESPISED AND TREATED UNFAIR, AS LIFE CHOKES MY DREAM AND I STRUGGLE FOR AIR, I WILL SPEAK OUT LOUD I DECREE AND DECLARE .

I WILL NOT QUIT

WE CAN DO IT

LET ME BE A MAN OF MEN TO PROTECT OUR LEGACY AND LEGEND

LET ME BE A PERSON OF INTEREST THAT WILL CREATE A POSITIVE PRESENCE

GIVEN THE CHANCE, I 'LL ENCOURAGE ALL CREATING OPPORTUNTIES

BEING ON GUARD FOR NEGATIVITY AFFECTING OUR COMMUNITY

TO SEEK HIGHER EDUCATION, GRANTS, SCHOLARSHIPS FOR TUITION

TAKING THE LEAD WITH ACTION, TO BRING IT INTO FRUITION

LEADING BY EXAMPLE TO CRUSH THE NOTION OF LESS AND LACK

BEING A MAN OF INTEGRITY, I' LL SUPPORT AND ALWAYS HAVE YOUR BACK

LOOKING AT THOSE WHO WOULD SAY, YOU CAN'T MAKE IT OUT OF THIS

STARING BACK AT THE NEGATIVE WITH BOLDNESS AND CONFIDENCE

TOGETHER WE CAN CHANGE HISTORY, ONE PERSON AT A TIME

ONLY BY JOINING HAND IN HAND WITH ALL OF MANKIND

MINDSETS MUST SHIFT, WITH THE COMMITMENT OF STICKING TO IT

DETERMINED WITH ONE VOICE; ALL SAYING WE CAN DO IT

SOUND THE ALARM

AS I SPEAK TO ONE I SPEAK TO ALL,

SOUND THE ALARM FOR THE CLARION CALL

DID YOU THINK THAT SUCCESS WOULD COME ALL OF A SUDDEN

AS IF PEOPLE WOULD LAG AROUND AND PROSPER HITTING SNOOZE BUTTONS

YOU HAVE BEEN MISINFORMED, MISLEAD BY LIES OF LUCK AND CHANCE

THINKING YOU'D WAKE UP WITH EVERYTHING WITHOUT WORKING A PLAN

WE NEED TO THINK BEFORE WE SPEAK, WAIT BEFORE WE ACT

OR BETTER YET REACT TO THE TRUTH, BASED OFF FACTS.

NOT GET INTO USELESS ARGUMENTS THAT WASTE PRECIOUS TIME

LETS STAND TO IMPROVE WHAT WE CAN AND USE OUR MINDS

AS I SPEAK TO ONE I SPEAK TO ALL,

SOUND THE ALARM FOR THE CLARION CALL

RING IT TO THE HIGHEST, UNTIL WE ALL GET OVER OUR DIFFERENCES

THAT CAUSES DIVISION BETWEEN US, BECAUSE OF PURE IGNORANCES

BEING THE FATHERS WE SHOULD BE, PARENTS AS ROLE MODELS

TO BE THE MOST IMPORTANT EXAMPLE, OUR KIDS WILL FOLLOW

WE'LL BLEED, CRY, AND GIVE UNTIL REVELATIONS ARE SEEN

SPEAKING LIFE INTO THEM ALL, SO THAT THEY CAN ACHIEVE ANYTHING

THEY SET THEIR HEART AND MIND TO DO WITH FOCUS AND VISION

LET'S GET IT DONE AND DO OUR PART TO ACCOMPLISH THE MISSION.

AS I SPEAK TO ONE I SPEAK TO ALL,

SOUND THE ALARM FOR THE CLARION CALL

MOTIVATION

PART 1

WHAT DRIVES YOU TO STAY THE COURSE, PRESSING PAST OPPOSITION

MOTIVATE YOURSELF WITH PASSION, MIXED WITH AMBITION

WHEN ALL OF THE FACTORS NEEDED, ARE PROPERLY INSTILLED

NOW THE STRATEGY FOR SUCCESS, WILL BE FULFILLED

MOTIVATION PUSHES YOU PAST THE MOST NEGATIVE OF THOUGHTS

BEFORE YOU START YOUR JOURNEY, CONSIDER ALL OF THE COSTS

NO ONE CAN PUT A LIMIT, ON WHAT YOU CAN ACHIEVE

NO ONE CAN MEASURE YOUR FAITH, AND WHAT YOU BELIEVE

TRUE MOTIVATION

MOTIVATED (PART 2)

THERE'S A CROSSROAD WE FACE, ON THE ROAD OF OUR DESTINATION

BE INTENT ON BEING CONSISTENT, COMMITTED WITH DEDICATION

FAILURE IS BEHIND YOU, ENCOURAGEMENT IS BY YOUR SIDE

STANDING STRONG AND DETERMINED, WITH DEFINITE PRIDE

ZOOM IN ON THE FINISH, THE PLACE YOU DESIRE SO MUCH

YOU'RE SO CLOSE TO THE GOAL, THERE'S NO THOUGHT OF GIVING UP

MOTIVATION IS REMEMBRING, YOUR WHAT AND YOUR WHY

GIVING ALL THAT IS WITHIN YOU, SO YOUR DREAM DOES NOT DIE

STAY MOTIVATED

WHO ARE YOU?

YESTERDAY IS GONE
TOMORROW IS NOT PROMISED
BUT TODAY, TODAY, TODAY
I AM_____?

WHAT ARE YOU?

FILL IN THE BLANK DAILY.

CHAPTER 4: FAMILY AND FUN

MOMMA

MY SON

MY DAUGHTER

A BROKEN HEARTED MAN

TRUTH FORUM FAMILY

PEANUT BUTTER/JELLY

NOW THAT'S FUNNY

MOMMA (I LOVE YOU)

MOMMA YOU SOWED INTO MY LIFE, A VISION AND A DREAM

AT A VERY EARLY AGE, YOU SAID I COULD ACCOMPLISH ANYTHING

I WAS THE TYPE OF KID, THAT WANTED TO DO IT ALL

AS I BEGAN TO GET OLDER, I STARTED TO FAIL AND FALL

PEER PRESSURE AND TEMPTATION, SLOWLY GOT THE BEST OF ME

THE MOTHER THAT YOU ARE, NEVER THOUGHT ANY LESS OF ME

I KNOW I BROUGHT SHAME AND CAUSED YOU TO HURT A LOT

IN SPITE OF ALL THE PAIN, YOUR LOVE FOR ME NEVER STOPPED

ALL THE THINGS YOU HAVE DONE COULD NEVER EVER BE REPLACED

MEMORIES OF YOU NURSING ME WITH 2ND DEGREE BURNS ON MY FACE

I COULD GO ON AND ON, EXPRESSING MY LOVE AND HONOR

HOPING YOU TRULY KNOW, THAT I REALLY LOVE YOU MOMMA.

MY SON

JUST TO BE MENTIONED WITH YOU, BRINGS ME GREAT JOY,

TO HAVE A PART IN GOD'S CREATION, IN HAVING A BOY,

MY MANCHILD, MY TWIN, BORN IN THIS SEASON

SON YOU ARE MY WHY, MY ROCK AND MY REASON.

WHEN I SEE YOU, I SEE THAT WE ARE ONE;

YOU ARE THE GREATEST GIFT TO ME, MY ONE, AND ONLY SON.

[I LOVE YOU SON].

MY DAUGHTER

MY DAUGHTER AND BABY, WITH DADDY'S EYES AND MY NOSE,

MY DAUGHTER YOU ARE A PRINCESS, DADDY'S QUEEN AT 3YRS OLD.

HOW BLESSED AM I, TO BEHOLD YOU AS MY CHILD

AFFIRMING YOUR GREATNESS EARLY, MAKES YOUR DADDY OH SO PROUD,

SO REMEMBER THROUGH OUT YOUR DAYS, ALL BECAUSE OF YOU,

WHEN THE DOCTOR DELIVERED MY BABY GIRL, DADDY REALLY LOVES YOU.

[LOVE YOU DAUGHTER]

A BROKEN HEARTED MAN

THE DISAPPOINTMENTS OF BETRAYAL, FEELING RIPPED AND TORN APART

ARE NOT EASILY DETECTED FROM A MAN WITH A BROKEN HEART

WE ARE TAUGHT TO BE STRONG AND HIDE OUR TRUE EMOTION

WHILE THERE'S A DECAY OF OUR FABRIC, LAYERED IN HEAVY CORROSION

WE LOVE HARD AND STRONG, OUR HEARTS DO BRUISE AND BLEED

MORE OFTEN WE COVER IT UP, IN ISOLATION WHEN WE GRIEVE

WE WILL GIVE OUR ALL AND DO OUR VERY BEST

ONLY TO SEE THERE ARE MANY MEN HURTING IN BROKENNESS

THIS IS NOT FOR SYMPATHY, OR FOR YOU TO FEEL SORRY FOR US

IT IS TRULY TO GIVE PERSPECTIVE, RELATING TO A DEEPER PART OF US

SO AS I WRITE THIS EXPRESSSION, I WANT YOU TO UNDERSTAND

HOW TO FULLY REGCONIZE, *A BROKEN HEARTED MAN*

TRUTH FORUM FAMILY

ITS 4: 45 IN THE AM, IT'S TIME FOR INTERCESSION

OH HOW GOD DISGUISED TRUTH FORUM AS MY BLESSING

SCROLLING THE FACEBOOK FEED, TO KILL TIME ON MY SHIFT

SEEING DEMACRUS'S POST ON PRAYER WAS A HIDDEN GIFT

I BEGAN TO LISTEN TO THE LINE, REALLY DIDN'T KNOW WHY

THE PRAYERS OF THE TRUTH FORUM, CARRIED ME THROUGH JULY

THEY WERE UNAWARE OF ME, BEING PRESENT ON THE LINE

NOT KNOWING HOW HURT I WAS, WAITING FOR PRAYER TIME

IT WAS JUST A FEW PEOPLE, LIKE NATALIE, FAITH, AND DAYA

AND THEN ON OTHER DAYS IT WAS DEMARCUS, LAVEYDA, AND AVA

THEN IT BEGAN TO EXPAND, WITH MANY OTHERS JOINING IN

NOW I TRULY CONSIDER THEM ALL, AS MY FAMILY AND MY FRIENDS

IT IS SO MANY NOW, I DON'T WANT TO MISS YOUR NAME

JUST KNOW SINCE OUR CONNECTION, LIFE WILL NEVER BE THE SAME

LOVE YOU TRUTH FORUM FAMILY

MIN. AVA BETHEL, SISTER LATRICE PAYEN, MIN. LAVEYDA PEARSON

EVG. DAYA RELLI, MIN. ERICKA CALDWELL-CLINCH, SIS. VERONICA LAMAR

SIS. RENESA COLLIER, EVG. JO GENOUS, SIS. KATHRYN HUDSON

SIS. LATRENDA SMALL, SIS. JACKIE YOUNG, SIS. COURTNEY JORDAN

SIS. SHANTELL MILLINGS, PASTOR INGER HANNA, MIN. LINDA SEARS

MIN. SHUNDA BROWN, REV. SHIRLEY BROWN, APOSTLE ROSE WHITE

MIN .SHANTEL CALLOWAY, MIN. VAL ANDERSON, MIN. KONJE BYRON

MIN. CORTES LEWIS, MIN.BETTY BROOKS, MIN. ANYA JAMES
MIN. KEISHA ARMSTRONG, SIS. JAMESE PATTERSON, PASTOR RHONDA F. LEWIS

MIN. DEMARCUS WILLIAMS, MIN. CHERYL COLEMAN

PEANUT BUTTER AND JELLY

PEANUT BUTTER AND JELLY, SEPARATE BUT TOGETHER

PEANUT BUTTER SAYS TO JELLY, I MAKE THIS SANDWICH BETTER

SO JELLY RESPONDS THAT IS TRUE, BUT I GIVE IT SWEETNESS AND TASTE

NOT TO MENTION I GO WELL WITH BISCUITS AND STILL BE IN PLACE

PEANUT BUTTER SAYS OK, CRACKERS AND US ARE GREAT SNACKS

SO JELLY ANSWER THIS QUESTION CAN YOU AND THE CRACKER DO THAT?

NO JELLY REPLIES, BUT I'M SOFT, GENTLE, AND CONSERVATIVE

CAN YOU THE SAME PEANUT BUTTER, JELLY IS THE # 1 PRESERVATIVE

NOW PEANUT BUTTER IS FURIOUS, BECAUSE JELLY MAKES A LOT OF SENSE

SO PEANUT BUTTER SAYS I'M IN COOKIES AND CAKES, PLUS I'M INTELLIGENT

SO JELLY SITS AND WAITS IN A JAR WITH NO RESPONSE

AND OFFERS A PEACE TREATY, KNOWING THERE'S A COMMON BOND

THEY KNOW BOTH OF THEM WILL BE EATEN IN AVERY SHORT TIME

THEY LOOK EACH OTHER IN THE FACE AND SAY WE ARE ONE OF A KIND

NOW THAT'S FUNNY

IMAGINE BEING A COMEDIAN, AND NO ONE LAUGHS AT YOUR JOKES,

OR SAYING YOU ARE A SINGER AND CANNOT SING A NOTE.

HAVE YOU EVER SPOKE OUT LOUD THINKING YOU'RE NOT BEING HEARD,

ONLY TO REALIZE SOMEONE WAS LISTENING AND NEVER SAID A WORD.

[NOW THAT'S FUNNY]

HAVE YOU EVER BEEN ON A DATE, WITH A BUDGET IN MIND

PRAYING WHEN YOU GET THE BILL, YOUR CARD WON'T BE DECLINED

YOU THINK THAT YOU ARE SMART AND NO ONE IS GREATER

THINK AGAIN SMARTY PANTS, YOU'RE NOT SMARTER THAN A 5TH GRADER

THINK ABOUT TRYING TO BE FUNNY, ONLY TO SEE THE JOKES ON YOU,

ADDING INSULT TO INJURY, ALL THE JOKES ARE TRUE.

[NOW THAT'S FUNNY]

THIS IS FOR US TO LOOSEN UP AND LIVE, LOVE AND LAUGH. LAUGHTER IS

GOOD FOR THE SOUL.

CHAPTER 5: CONVICTIONS

WE OWE YOU

WARNING SIGNS

SILENT KILLER

TRANSPARENCY

IT'S MY CHOICE

THE RAIN

FORGIVENESS

WE OWE YOU

TO OUR CHILDREN, OUR SONS AND DAUGHTERS. PLEASE ALLOW US AS FATHERS TO REPENT FOR OUR SELFISHNESS. WE HAVE WRONGED YOU BY THINKING ONLY OF OURSELVES, TREATING YOU LIKE AN OBLIGATION AND NOT LIKE OUR OWN CHILDREN. PLEASE ALLOW US TO BE A PART OF THE FUTURE, KNOWING WE HAVE MISSED THE PAST.

WE WILL NOT MAKE ANY EXCUSES FOR OUR BEHAVIOR, BECAUSE WE DON'T CONTROL LIFE, PEOPLE, OR CIRCUMSTANCES. WE DO THOUGH, CONTROL HOW WE RESPOND TO THEM. AS WE MOVE FORWARD, WE PRAY FOR YOUR FORGIVENESS AND A PIECE OF YOUR LIFE THAT YOU WOULD BE WILLING TO SHARE. PLEASE KNOW THAT WE LOVE YOU AND WILL DO OUR BEST TO SHOW IT WITH ACTIONS. WE WILL BE, WHAT WE ARE YOUR (FATHERS). PLEASE FORGIVE US

WARNING SIGNS

WILL YOU PRAY THAT ALL MY HAND TOUCHES   BE PROSPEROUS,

ALTERNATIVELY, DO YOU PREY AGAINST ME, TO RENDER ME POWERLESS

DO YOU REALLY LOVE THE PERSON I AM, AND STRIVE TO BE

ALTERNATIVELY, DO YOU HATE MY PRESENCE; SLANDER MY NAME WITH JEALOUSY

WILL YOU CATCH WHEN I FALL, HOLD ME WHEN I'M AFFLICTED

ON THE OTHER HAND, DO YOU BETRAY WITH KISSES, SENDING ME AWAY CONVICTED

MY HOPE IS THAT YOU'RE FOR ME, UNITED WITH ONE HEART AND MIND,

WITH WISDOM I AM CAREFUL, TO DISCERN THE WARNING SIGNS.

SILENT KILLER

Memo: To all Women, The greatest enemy a Man faces is Silence. Yes, silence, silence has destroyed and killed people, marriages, relationships, families, and plans. Listen, please allow Men to express, and relieve themselves from the pressures of Life. I/We promise to never hurt or harm [You], demean or degrade [You] control or restrict [You] disrespect or dishonor [You] .This is for all of you [Women] to better understand Us. We are not weak if we Cry [we have emotions] we are not useless if we Fail [Only if we quit] We need Support, Honor, Respect, and Our Voices to be heard .We love you [Women]...

TRANSPARENCY

I SPEAK ON BEHALF OF ALL MEN, WHO WOULD SHARE THE SAME THOUGHTS,

SENTIMENTS AND REMORSE. WOMEN/ LADIES WE ARE TRULY SORRY FOR

ALL THE LIES, HEARTACHES, DECEPTION, MANIPULATIONS, ABUSE, NEGLECT,
SEIFISHNESS

BEING CONTROLLING AND THE UNFAITHFULNESS. NOT TO MENTION, CAUSING
HARM AND ATTACKING

THE VERY ESSENCE OF YOUR LIFE (SELF ESTEEM), IN WHICH YOU NEED THE
MOST. I PROMISE YOU THIS IS NOT FOR SELF PROMOTION OR TO GAIN
ANYTHING. OUR HEARTS HAVE BEEN CRYING

OUT FOR YEARS CONCERNING THIS ISSUE. PLEASE FORGIVE US FOR ALL THESE
THINGS PLEASE.

HOPEFULLY WITH THIS YOU WILL BE ABLE TO HEAL AND REGAIN WHAT WAS
TAKEN FROM YOU

THAT IS [YOU] YOUR VERY BEING. WE DECLARE THAT _ALL OF YOU_ ARE ROYAL
QUEENS IN THE EARTH

YOU ARE GODS BEST CREATION... WE LOVE YOU AND GOD BLESS.

IT'S MY CHOICE

IT'S MY CHOICE TO LOVE AND NOT HATE PEOPLE

TO EXPRESS THE GREATER GOOD TO OVERCOME THE EVIL

IT'S MY CHOICE TO FORGIVE AND FORGET THE PAST

TO BE FREED FROM THE ANGER CHOOSING NOT TO BE MAD

IT'S MY CHOICE NOT TO BE BITTER, BUT BETTER

RESPONDING IN A MANNER THAT BRINGS US CLOSER TOGETHER

IT'S MY CHOICE NOT TO QUIT AND NOTHING WILL STOP IT

MY DREAM BECOMING REALITY, BECAUSE IT'S NOT AN OPTION

IT'S MY CHOICE, TO CHOOSE THE COMPANY I KEEP

SEEKING TO WIN ALWAYS, NEVER ACCEPTING DEFEAT

IT'S MY CHOICE TO MAKE SURE MY INFLUENCES ARE STABLE

NEVER MAKING TRUE THE STEREOTYPES AND LABELS

IT'S MY CHOICE TO BE FREE AND NOT CAPTIVE

BY THE THOUGHT OF BEING PRODUCTIVE WITHOUT BEING PRO-ACTIVE

IT'S MY CHOICE, MY LIFE, AND MY VOICE,

CONTROLLED ONLY BY ME, BECAUSE IT IS MY CHOICE.

THE RAIN

JUST THE SOUND OF RAIN, BRINGS A TRANQUIL EFFECT OF STILLNESS

AS THE DROPS HIT THE GROUND, THE RAIN IS HEALING THE EARTH'S ILLNESS

RAIN BRINGS GROWTH TO US ALL, THE SEED AND IT'S GRAIN

NOTHING WILL GROW WITHOUT THE MOISTURE FROM THE RAIN

RAIN IS SATURATING, LIKE A DRENCHING DOWN POUR

RAIN IS ESSENTIAL TO THE HARVEST IN ADDING MUCH MORE

SO ASK FOR THE RAIN, LIVE FOR THE RAIN,

WELCOME THE RAIN, AND RECEIVE THE RAIN.

FORGIVENESS

FORGIVENESS IS A POWERFUL FORCE. IT UNLOCKS THE CAPTIVIVTY OF THE PERSON THAT GRANTS THE FORGIVENESS. I CAN ONLY IMAGINE WHAT SOME HAVE BEEN THROUGH. SOME ISSUES AND CIRCUMSTANCES THAT ARE SO PAINFUL, JUST A MOMENT OF THE THOUGHTS WOULD BRING TERRIBLE MEMORIES. FORGIVENESS IS FOR ALL, BUT ESPECIALLY FOR THE PERSON THAT WAS VICTIMIZED. IT IS NOT EASY TO FORGIVE AND NEVER THINK THAT IT WILL BE. IT'S NECESSARY FOR THE FREEDOM OF ONE'S MIND TO FUNCTION AND TO CONTINUE TO RECEIVE THE QUALITY OF LIFE THAT PERSON DESERVES. SO BE FREE, FREE TO BE FORGIVEN AND GRANT FORGIVENESS. GOD BLESS.

CHAPTER 6: UNCONDITIONAL LOVE

GRASS AND WEEDS

WHO CAN SAY

LIFE

SUNFLOWER

LOVE

MY WIFE MY RIB

I PROMISE

GRASS AND WEEDS (THE GRASS IS NOT GREENER)

A BLADE OF GRASS, WOW, HOW PRECIOUS IS THE SIGHT

A WEED THAT RESEMBLES THE GRASS IS EXPOSED IN THE LIGHT

A GRASS SEED THAT IS PLANTED, REPRODUCES AFTER ITS KIND

WEEDS ARE DEFINED AS TROUBLEMAKERS, TRYING TO CHOKE YOUR VINE

THE WEED COMES IN DISGUISE TO MIMMICK AND GAIN ACCESS

WHILE ONLY SEEKING TO GAIN FROM THE GRASS SEED'S SUCCESS

SO BE CAREFUL AND WATCH, FOR THE DEADLY SNEAKY WEED

ALWAYS REMEMBER YOUR GRASS, IS THE ONLY GRASS YOU'LL NEED.

THE MORAL TO THIS POEM. THE GRASS REPRESENTS THE GOOD HUSBAND, WIFE AND FAMILY YOU HAVE. THE WEEDS ARE OUTSIDERS TRYING TO PRETEND TO BE WHAT THEY'RE NOT. BE A CULTIVATOR OF YOUR GRASS AND GET WEED KILLER (LOVE) FOR THE WEEDS

WHO CAN SAY

WHO CAN SAY, WHAT LOVE REALLY FEELS LIKE,

YOU CAN SAY THAT IT FEELS SAFE, WARM, AND NICE.

WHO CAN SAY, THAT A DREAM WON'T COME TRUE,

THEY CAN SAY WHAT THEY WILL; I SAY MY DREAM IS YOU.

WORDS CAN EXPRESS FEELINGS, BUT ACTIONS ADD VALUE,

THE WORD THAT COMES TO MY MIND IS I'M SO GLAD I HAVE YOU.

SO WHO CAN SAY, WHAT SHOULD AND SHALL BE,

NO ONE CAN SAY THE THINGS MY HEART CAN SEE.

THE PAST PAINS AND THE HURTS, HAS YOUR HEART CRYING OUT,

FOR A COMFORTING LOVE, THAT IS TRUE, LOYAL, AND DEVOUT.

ADORATION AND HONOR IS GIVEN TO YOU MY QUEEN,

LOVE AND AFFECTION, SHOWN BOLDLY FROM THIS KING.

WOMEN ARE LONGING FOR THE REAL MEN TO STAND,

WHAT A PRIVILEGE BESTOWED UPON ME, TO CARRY THIS COMMAND.

SO WHO CAN SAY?.......I CAN...YOU CAN... WE CAN

LIFE

LIFE IS LIKE THE WIND, EVER CHANGING AS IT COMES IT GOES

WITH SEASONS OF MOUNTAIN HIGHS, DEPTHS OF VALLEY LOWS

BUT REMEMBER THE SPECIAL DAYS, CHERISH AND GUARD THEM CLOSE

MORE THAN ANYTHING EXPRESS THE LOVE, TO THOSE YOU VALUE MOST

TOMORROW IS NOT PROMISED AND AT ANY SECOND LIFE COULD END

SO ENJOY EACH MOMENT AND MAKE THE MOST OF LIFE MY FRIEND

LIFE IS LIKE THE SUN, IT SHINES AND GOES AWAY

SO PLEASE MAKE IT A PRIORITY TO ENJOY LIFE TODAY

SUNFLOWER

AS THE SUN SETS AND MY DAY COMES TO AN END,

WHISPERS FROM YOUR VOICE GIVES ME COMFORT DEEP WITHIN.

THE BALANCE I NEED BETWEEN DISCIPLINE, DEDICATION, AND DEVOTION,

OFTENTIMES IS GENTLY GRACED BY THE SOUL OF YOUR EMOTIONS.

COMPLETE I FEEL, COMPLIMENTED I AM, CONFIRMED BY YOUR SMILE,

APPOINTED, ELECTED, AND VIRTUOUS, PROVERBS 31 STYLE.

TO WAIT SO LONG, YOUR LOVE IS MY SONG,

TO BE SO FREE, KNOWING YOU ARE WITH ME.

POETIC I EXPRESS, OUTWARDLY THIS VERY HOUR,

GRATITUDE, ADMIRATION, AND LOVE FOR YOU SUNFLOWER.

LOVE

A LOVE THAT CONQUERS IS A LOVE THAT'S PURE,

A LOVE THAT KNOWS IS A LOVE THAT'S SURE.

A LOVE THAT PROTECTS KEEPS YOU SAFE FROM HARM,

A LOVE TO RESTORE AND HOLDS YOU WARM.

A LOVE THAT'S UNSELFISH, IS A LOVE THAT GIVES,

A LOVE THAT WILLS TO DIE, SO YOU CAN LIVE.

LOVE SO INNOCENT YOU CAN'T OR WILL NOT DEFINE IT,

IT DEFINES YOU, ONLY WHEN YOU FIND IT.

THIS LOVE FEELS WHOLE, COMPLETE, AND DESIGNED,

A LOVE CONNECTED AND PERFECTED BY [JESUS] IS TRULY DIVINE.

MY WIFE MY RIB

MY WIFE MY RIB TO YOU I PROMISE,

TO ALWAYS BE KIND, GENTLE, AND HONEST.

MY WIFE MY RIB TO YOU I GIVE,

THIS DAY MY ALL THROUGH YOU I 'LL LIVE.

MY WIFE MY RIB MY LOVE, MY FRIEND;

FATHER, MOTHER, FAMILY, AND CHILDREN.

MY WIFE, MY RIB, MY SHOULDER, MY EAR,

TO YOU I SHARE MY LIFE MY DEAR.

MY WIFE, MY RIB, HELP MEET, AND GOOD THING

FINDING YOU GAVE ME FAVOR IN ALL YOU BRING.

MY WIFE, MY RIB, OUR DESTINY WAS FORMED,

WAY IN HEAVEN BEFORE WE WERE BORN.

MY WIFE MY RIB LOVELY AND UNIQUE,

ALL WRAPPED IN ONE WOMAN YOU ARE COMPLETE.

MY WIFE, MY RIB, SPECIAL AND SET APART,

MY WIFE, MY RIB, MY LOVE, MY HEART

I PROMISE

I PROMISE TO CULTIVATE A LIFE OF HAPPINESS AND CHERISH MY TREASURE

I PROMISE YOUR LOVE WILL BE PRIORITY, MY MOST IMPORTANT ENDEAVOR

I PROMISE TO BIND MY HEART AND SOUL IN CONNECTION TO YOURS

I PROMISE TO LISTEN, UNDERSTAND, AND FIGHT SO WE'LL WIN THE WAR

I PROMISE TO BE FAITHFUL, HONEST, AND TRUE, LOVING BEYOND CAPACITY

I PROMISE TO REACH DEEP INSIDE OF ME TO MAKE SURE YOU'RE HAPPY

I PROMISE AS A MAN YOUR HUSBAND, TO LEAD BY GODS DIRECTION

I PROMISE THE WORD WILL COUNSEL US LEAVING NO ROOM FOR DECEPTION

I PROMISE TO LIVE A LIFE WORTHY OF ACCOUNTABILITY

I PROMISE TO BE A GREAT FATHER TAKING MY RIGHTFUL PLACE IN SOCIETY

I PROMISE I'M OPEN TO YOUR INPUT AND ADVICE FOR OUR DESTINY

I PROMISE YOUR LIFE WILL BE ALL THAT YOU WANT, WITH ME

I PROMISE

CHAPTER 7: WORSHIP

FOREVER FREE

I NEED THEE (PART 1)

I NEED THEE (PART 2)

GOD INDEED

GRACE

FAITHFUL

SILENCE

FOREVER FREE

FOREVER FREE FROM THE BONDAGE OF CHAINS THAT HELD ME,

FOREVER FREE FROM THE PATH OF DESTRUCTION THAT DERAILED ME.

FOREVER FREE FROM THE PENALTY OF THE ULTIMATE DEATH SENTENCE,

FOREVER FREE FROM THE CHARGES OF SIN THROUGH FORGIVENESS AND REPENTANCE.

FOREVER FREE FROM DECEPTION, THAT BRINGS LUST AND TEMPTATION,

FOREVER FREE TO BELIEVE IN OUR LORD JESUS AND RECEIVE HIS SALVATION.

FOREVER FREE TO PRAISE, WORSHIP, ADORE, AND ADMIRE,

FOREVER FREE FROM DAMNATION, DEATH, HELL, AND THE LAKE OF ETERNAL FIRE.

FOREVER FREE TO INHERIT THE GIFT OF EVERLASTING LIFE

FOREVER FREE ALL DUE TO THE DEATH, BURIAL, AND RESSURECTION

OF OUR LORD AND SAVIOR JESUS CHRIST. I'M FOREVER FREE.

I NEED THEE (PART 1)

WHEN BURDENS GET HEAVY AND MY TRIALS SEEM MUCH,

I REACH OUT FOR STRENGTH AND GET IT FROM YOUR TOUCH.

SEE I COULD PAINT THE PICTURE OF ALL ROSES AND PLEASURE,

TRUTH BE TOLD IT GETS ROUGH AND LONELY, BUT IT DOES GET BETTER.

I NEED THEE LORD, YES LORD I REALLY DO,

I NEED YOU LORD TO HELP AND BRING ME THROUGH.

IT'S PAINFUL AND HURTING, THESE TEARS WON 'T GO AWAY,

WEEPING ENDURES FOR A NIGHT; BRING THE JOY YOU PROMISED TODAY.

I'M AT MY END, I'M ALL OUT OF EMOTIONS TO FEEL,

DO A WORK IN ME LORD, AND LET IT BE YOUR PERFECT WILL.

LOOKING TO THE HILLS, ASKING FOR MERCY ON ME

I CAN'T MAKE WITHOUT LORD, I NEED THEE

I NEED THEE (PART 2)

AS WE LIVE, WE ENDURE, MANY TRIALS THAT CAUSE DOUBT

SOME DAYS ARE SO DARK AND DIM, AS IF THE LIGHT IS ALMOST OUT

BEING MISUNDERSTOOD, EVEN FOR GOOD WE INTEND TO DO

BESEECHING MY FATHER WITH ALL I HAVE, DECLARING I NEED YOU

PERIL IS AT MY LEFT, SICKNESS AND DEATH IS ON THE RIGHT

THE HURTS OF LIVING HERE, IT'S HARD TO GET THROUGH THE NIGHT

SO KNOW THIS LORD PLEASE, LIKE THE THIEF REMEMBER ME

YOU ARE MY STRENGTH WHEN I'M WEAK, LORD I NEED THEE

GOD INDEED

GOD IS MY REFUGE, WHOM SHALL I FEAR,

I DON'T HAVE TO LOOK FOR HIM BECAUSE HE 'S ALWAYS HERE.

OUR TESTS AND TRIALS COME ONLY TO STRENGTHEN OUR FAITH,

A SIGN OF SPIRITUAL GROWTH GIVEN BY GODS GRACE.

JUST THINK FOR A MOMENT, IN TIMES LOST AND CONFUSED,

HOW HE CAME IN THE MOMENT, YOU THOUGHT YOU WERE THROUGH.

BRAND NEW MERCIES GIVEN BY HIS UNDYING LOVE,

AVAILABLE TO ANYONE THAT LOOKS TO THE HILLS ABOVE.

SOMETIMES HE SEEMS SO FAR, YOUR HOPE GETS SMALL AND THIN,

BEING ALPHA AND OMEGA, THE BEGINNING, AND YOUR END.

SO UNDERSTAND YOUR HOPE AND FAITH IS ALL YOU NEED

GOD IS OUR REFUGE, OUR EVERYTHING INDEED.

GRACE

BECAUSE OF GRACE, TODAY I'M FREE TO LIVE,

BECAUSE GRACE CAME WILLING TO FORGIVE.

BECAUSE GRACE TOOK MY PLACE OF GUILT AND SHAME,

BECAUSE GRACE SHOWED UP, IN JESUS NAME.

BECAUSE GRACE SAID NO, DON'T KILL HIM,

THAT SAME GRACE THAT SHOUTED FATHER PLEASE FORGIVE THEM.

GRACE THAT GOES BEYOND HUMAN COMPREHENSION,

GRACE THAT WAS BEATEN BEYOND HUMAN RECOGNITION.

CAN YOU IMAGINE THE AGONY OF THE CROSS,

GRACE WRAPPED HIMSELF IN FLESH TO PAY THE HIGHEST COST.

THEY SAY IT'S AMAZING, I TOTALLY AGREE,

GRACE THAT WAS GIVEN TO ALL OF US, TOTALLY FREE.

I UNDERSTAND, HOW TO SHOW MY GRATITUDE,

SUBMITTING MYSELF TO YOU WITH A RIGHTEOUS ATTITUDE.

THIS GRACE I'VE GOT MEET HIM AND SEE IT FACE TO FACE

TO SHOUT HALLELUJAH, THANK YOU JESUS FOR YOUR AMAZING GRACE.

FAITHFUL

WHEN I THINK OF YOU I'M CAPTIVATED, AT TIMES I GET SPEECHLESS

KNOWING YOU ARE THE ONLY ONE THAT CAN BRING ME TO COMPLETENESS

HOW I THINK BACK, I REJECTED YOU SO MANY TIMES

BUT YOU NEVER GAVE UP ON ME, HAVING MY BEST INTEREST IN MINE

SO I WANTED TO SAY THANK YOU TO SHOW YOU I'M GRATEFUL

BECAUSE YOUR LOVE IS UNCONDITIONAL, LORD YOU ARE SO FAITHFUL

LOVE YOU..........

SILENCE

SILENCE IS GOLDEN. IT SPEAKS TO THE INNER MAN. IT ALLOWS YOU TO HEAR THE STILL SMALL VOICE OF GOD. IT'S A PLACE WHERE PEACE RESIDES AND CHAOS IS PUT AWAY. YEARN TO GET AWAY, BE STILL, AND SIT SILENTLY BEFORE THE LORD. LET THE SILENCE BE YOUR COMPANIONSHIP, WHEN NO ONE IS AROUND. SIT, THINK AND LISTEN. THERE IS PEACE IN CENTER OF SILENCE.

GOD BLESS

THANK YOU LORD FOR BLESSING ME TO COMPLETE THIS, WITHOUT YOU I AM NOTHING. THANK YOU TO MY FAMILY AND FRIENDS IN ST. LOUIS, TUPELO, TOLEDO, MIAMI, AND CALIFORNIA. I WOULD ESPECIALLY LIKE TO THANK MY MOTHER, COOKIE, CHARLONDA, COUSIN MILLIE AND JEFFRY. TO TEYSHANA "TW" WILEY FOR YOUR HELP AND SUPPORT , YOU ARE A GOD SENT LOVE YA; ATTORNEY DAVID AND MRS. SCHULTZ , RICHARD BROOKS,TERRON AND SHURETA MORRIS, JOLENA JOHNSON FOR BELIEVING IN ME, JOLENE JOHNSON FOR SPEAKING IT, YOLANDA YAVETT PARKER , TISHA DANIELS, TISHA WACAYS, PASTOR GARRETT AND PSALMIST GINA LLOYD AND LOVE IN THE WORLD OF CHRISTIANITY; TIFFANY SHANNON, LATANGELA ROGERS, SHIRLEY SMITH-TRIPLETT, ST. LOUIS COUNTY LIBRARY, LANA ROBAIN, SION JOHNSON-JACKSON,   PASTOR MORGAN, PASTOR MARK AND TINA GRIMES, D' ANDRE BRODERICK, RONETHIA CURTIS

LISA S. MACK, TASHUNA RAY, MARY BANKS, ARIAN TYSON, CORTES (BABY SIS) LEWIS, RENESA, VAL, AND KATHY, JASMYNE HINSON, TANYA JONES, DEANNA CHURCH, AVA, SHUNDA, MOMMA SHIRLEY AND THE TRUTH FORUM AGAIN, LASHANDRA SIMPSON, BISHOP SCOTT AND 1ST LADY SCOTT AND THE BELIEVER'S TEMPLE FAMILY, PASTOR JEFFERSON AND GRACE SCHOOL OF MINISTRY, ELDER (UNCLE) JOE POLLACK, CANDICE SPANN , ADRIANNE D. HUTCHINS AND ALL THAT I KNOW.

LOVE YOU ALL AND ENJOY, GOD BLESS